PICTOPLASMA 2
CONTEMPORARY CHARACTER DESIGN

EARLY 21ST CENTURY
ABOUT JAPANESE CHARACTER CULTURE

by Takashi Murakami

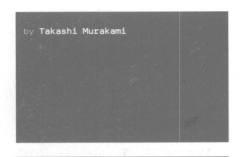

Takashi Murakami is an internationally acclaimed Japanese artist.
His "superflat" manifesto challenges the traditional boundaries between classical Japanese art and contemporary Japanese animation.

Japanese people are confounded to see that modern Japan has come so far as to have a system involving characters and realize that these characters have become a real "culture" rooted in the Japanese heart.

There is a theory that the Japanese characteristic of "communication weakness" between people is one of the reasons for the acceleration of character culture in post-war Japan, especially since the 1990's. In modern Japan efforts to communicate with closely exchanged opinions is not emphasized in reality. This root goes back to the way Japanese culture got established after its defeat in the Pacific War. In other words, under the mechanism where the top of every hierarchy was established outside of the Japanese sphere it became difficult for the Japanese to create their own hierarchy. For example in human relationships, in order to understand the personality it is more popular to character-type them as the perky main character, the prefect-like accommodating girlfriend character, the twisted character, the chubby character, the doctor (smart) character, the picked-on character, and so on, rather than having a strict top to bottom hierarchy system. A perfect example of this can be found in the character setting of the game and animation, "Pocket Monster." Although there are over three hundred types of elaborately defined character personalities, even within that huge variety, the hierarchy structure with an absolute top to bottom axis is very weak. On the contrary, even the weak characters hold a trump card giving them the potential for a one-shot reversal of fortune. In some ways one completed form of the worldview that the

post-war Japanese have reached is reflected here. At the same time because Japan is a "polytheistic" rather than "monotheistic" country there originally might have been a cultural background allowing for the large variety mentioned above.

Let me explain the history of post-war "on-site" which created such a historical structure. Japan's animation and character cultures are closely entwined. Even now, animation projects are produced one after another and tied up with toy companies that develop products. Ranging from traditional toys and elaborately duplicated plastic models to card games and computer games, these products have advanced as "promotion media" to get across the quality of character images and toys themselves. This originates in America. In the process of how Japanese character culture has advanced this far is the saturation of post-war American animation and importing countless numbers of corporate identities and characters that emerged in every kind of product advertisements such as food products in the American consumer society.

The post-war Japanese adored novelty goods and merchandise promotion designs imported from victorious America as a "dream from overseas" and they quickly penetrated into the culture. With this influence, Japan's own advertising characters sprouted like mushrooms. Currently existing characters such as the Fujiya pastry company's "PEKO-chan" and Marukome Miso's "MARUKOME-kun" were born in 1950, five years after the end of the war. Furthermore corporate icons for companies such as Matsushita Electric Industrial's (National/Panasonic) "National Kid" and Toshiba Electric Industries' "Kousoku Esper"

were made into live-action for children's television shows. Through translating imported character culture, Japanese started linking with a media who pushed new developments. This main media was indeed television animation.

On January 1st, 1963, the first black and white television animation went on the air. The hugely popular genius comic writer Osamu Tezuka took matters into his own hands, establishing Mushi Productions, an animation studio. With the groundbreaking TV animation "Astroboy" he opened history's curtain. Tezuka set animation production costs cheap because he was desperate to do TV animation. This has created a harsh working environment for successive on-site animators, and such a grossly underpaid work environment has not yet been corrected. However, you could also say that this low budget production system supported animation's development so that today it has advanced as a culture that has competitive power in the world animation market.

Once Mushi Production charged into TV animation, the long-established theater animation production studio Toei Douga (the present Toei Animation), also jumped aboard. They began producing pieces by delving into the original concepts of Hanna-Barbera, the famous American television animation team known for "Tom and Jerry" and "The Wacky Races". Toei Douga's first TV animation "Space Patrol Hopper", was a complete takeoff of Hanna-Barbera's "Space Family Robinson". This is also evident in the later-produced "Hustle Punch", a slapstick animation with characters designed by Yasuji Mori. Since then, Mushi Production and Toei Animation

have become the two major players in Japan's animation scene, having a major influence even now as the genesis of Japanese animation.

From the 80's onward, character culture developed further in the Japanese cutting-edge realm of the television game. Popular characters such as "Super Mario Brothers", "Sonic the Hedgehog" and "Dragon Quest" emerged as "dot image" graphics moving inside the games eventually evolving enough to be able to "portray" characters. Later, through renewal of game technology and improvements in game hardware infrastructure, more realistic characters reappeared on the screens. With the GameBoy kids could always carry with them and its representative game "Pocket Monster", the characters started achieving a quality so people could emotionally connect with them. Disregarding "Pocket Monster's" global saturation in the late 90's, the characters roaming around inside the games have completely turned into the pronouns of Japanese character culture.

Furthermore the unique character business like Sanrio's "Hello Kitty" has started to grow in Japan. The "Hello Kitty" character is "created purely for merchandise purposes" with no roots in animation or picture books. In the beginning its worldview closely resembled Dick Bruna's "Miffy", and appeared to be riding on the latter's coattails. However, even if picture books are published or animations are produced, "Hello Kitty's" uniqueness exists within denial of any specific stories, the character is itself. Sanrio expansive merchandise production IS the life of "Hello Kitty".

"Hello Kitty's" success led to the breakout of

companies producing characters such as "TarePanda", "Kogepan" and "Sushi Azarashi" with no links to original comics or merchandise promotion but rather as complete independent businesses. Those artificially created characters by such makers first test the characters popularity and give life to only those who survive the screening, which is a reverse method of traditional character development. At the apex of the character era, Japan is now known as a "character superpower." Various characters are bustling everywhere. Whether walking the street, watching TV or checking out a cellular phone idling screen, Japan is awash with characters. Cellular phones are adorned with character wallpaper, straps and stickers. Character prize giveaways sit on work desks while a huge number of various sized stuffed characters are displayed at home. According to the BANDAI Character Research Lab, 84% of the Japanese population own some form of character merchandise. Even among senior citizens the rate is as high as 65%. The order or place of the character's emergence continues to change in each case.

Presently the most happening place of birth for the character as a new movement is on the Internet in the form of "ASCII art" (emoticon). AA (ASCII art) originally indicated images literally created with ASCII (single-byte) characters. The origin goes back to America 20 years ago where the set of characters ":-)" was used as a smiley mark. "ASCII art" is "emoticon" created with combinations of symbols and characters that emerged from the saturated Internet and e-mail culture. Initially treated as "a casual emotional expression" attached to the end of sentences, many complex structures have begun to appear lately. Especially well-known in Japan, are the popular characters "Mona" and "Giko Cat" which appear on the giant discussion board called "2channel", a website based on rumors and hot gossip. Although "Mona" and "Giko Cat" are "ASCII art", their special thread stands out on the discussion board, several different versions are invented daily and even many related home pages have been created. The position of "Mona" and "Giko Cat" have distinct differences from the characters for animation-line merchandise as a premise or those that came out in the world for pure business purposes such as "Hello Kitty" as mentioned earlier. That is, they do not have merchandising as a premise but are born as free expression symbols and live in the area untouchable by marketing. The "2channel" character "Giko Cat" episode reiterates this stance. In this incident, "Giko Cat" was nearly registered as a trademark by a toy manufacturer "TAKARA Co., Ltd."

While searching the Patent Office home page for "Giko Cat" at 18:00 on June 2nd, 2002, a 2channel user discovered that TAKARA Co., Ltd. had registered this character as a trademark in March of the same year and reported it on 2channel's "News Flash Board" (http://news4.2ch.net/news/). The information debut on 2channel quickly spread to other bulletins such as the "Mona board", triggering especially strong reactions in people who expressed concern, anger and sadness about "Giko Cat" becoming commercialized by TAKARA. So 2channel's massive BBS joined in, showing the image of Giko Cat chained by TAKARA on its top page. Net users rebelled hard establishing websites to "protest against TAKARA" on free web spaces online. Voices

criticizing TAKARA went on and on. TAKARA, feeling a sense of crisis over the situation, swiftly issued a statement of apology to the 2channel users and withdrew the trademark application at 16:00 on the 3rd, just one day after the uproar.

TAKARA explained the situation leading up to the trademark application as such: "'Giko Cat' wasn't copyrighted so we considered merchandising it upon trademark registration." However when the trademark application was exposed on June 2nd, a "considerable" (quote by said corporation) amount of protest mail surged in so they figured out that "even though the trademark registration held no legal problems, as a realistic issue, commercialization would be difficult due to overwhelming criticism." They withdrew the application because "it was imprudent."

Information once it appears on the net is capable of limitless "infinite proliferation" functioning as characters that anyone can easily enjoy on the desktop or on the net with a quick copy & paste.

With the will of leaving the character copyright holder borderline concept vague, the characters secure the freedom to stay unbound earning the broadness.

As a symbol of AA, "Mona" and "Giko Cat's" presence is showing one of the answers for the birth of characters and its way of living in the present progressive form, having been born in Japan where character procreation has gone all the way.

At the opposite end of the spectrum copyright terms were extended and amended for an extremely well known American character icon under the Copyright Term Extension Act. This obsession toward business based on "copy-

right", and going to such lengths to claim it, reaches the national level only in America that considers the information industry its main power. The aforementioned "Giko Cat" case and prolonged copyright awarded to "the well known icon" in question is a mirror image. "What are the characters' rights?" The search in the name of copyright for the closer connection point to society will occur more and more.

The major roles of the Japanese characters I have introduced, whether it is "Pokemon" or "Giko Cat", after all, play the role as "communication tools." To accelerate the previously mentioned "TarePanda" boom, the media so incessantly drove home the "efficacy" point as a "healing product" that it drew attention as a communication mediator from children to businessmen beyond generations. Meanwhile, looking overseas, Sanrio's "Hello Kitty" is bigger in America than in Japan, its country of origin. This makes sense as well. America's recent racial shift with Latinos outnumbering African-Americans and an increasing Asian population indicates the background for accepting animation more. A minority in the early 90's when the Japanimation boom began, they are now close to becoming a majority. As communication tools moving beyond race, animation and characters are meeting their potential. Transcending a communication gap Japanese can't possibly imagine, the common language developed by the "communication weak" Japanese is becoming useful.

I believe that characters will continue to repeatedly transform in the future, creating areas where new characters can live.

ASCII ART

What is presently called "ASCII art (AA from hereon after)" in Japan is primarily created with "double-byte characters (not ASCII or single-byte characters)", so strictly speaking, it is not composed with "ASCII" but it is known as such.

The reason behind why American born AA has so much variation in Japan is due to the "double-byte character." In Europe and the United States (including the Western European language sphere), you can input single-byte characters only. Depending on the language, extra characters can also be typed in but like the accent in French and the German umlaut not much variation exists. On the con-

trary, in Japanese not only single-byte but double-byte characters can be used as well. (For example, when typing Hiragana or Chinese characters.) Double-byte characters have a great variation so that when you want to express "this kind of facial expression/shape", it is easier to find suitably shaped characters.

For example:

```
           Λ__Λ          Λ__Λ
  д      目 ̄   ( ´ ∀ ` )     ( · ∀ · )
              (      )      (      )
              │ │ │        │ │ │
              (__) _)      (__) _)
```

open mouth   **tea**   **This is Mona**   .

Figure 1   Figure 2   Figure 3   Figure 4

```
         -=   Λ__Λ
      -=≡  ( ﾟдﾟ )
         -= ( つ─っ
      -=≡ │   │/
     -=≡  / / │)
       ◎─＼ )─┴─◎
```

Figure 5

Skipping over other elements that pushed its development, this is a new character category extremely developed through the unification of a technical background and the Japanese love toward characters.

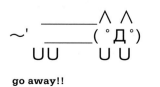

```
         _____Λ Λ
  ~' _____( ﾟДﾟ)
    UU      U U
```

go away!!

Figure 6

Σ (ﾟдﾟ|||) Oh my God!

Oh my (ﾟДﾟ;) God!

Here it comes ─────(ﾟ∀ﾟ)───── ！！！！

Figures 7

CHARACTER ASSASSINATIONS

by Philip Hunt
Studio aka

Philip Hunt is a Director and Creative Director at
Studio aka in London, UK.

www.studioaka.co.uk

It wears me out to think about the number of times I've read the same candid instruction heading a script: "This commercial features fresh and innovative animation and character design in a style that has not been seen before." Such promissory hyperbole elicits a dread filled allure time and again. Don't get me wrong, but it's simply not possible to be entirely comfortable with the commercial process when you are constantly discarding everything you have done before. Whilst the great thing about expressing commercial narratives is that we rarely repeat ideas, the need to continually reinvent ourselves makes for an uneasy relationship. Maybe that's what keeps it interesting.

As a method of articulating information in an engaging manner, character animation naturally provides advertisers a way to impart messages with an apparent humanity that wears its heart if not on its sleeve, than at least in its back pocket. Though faking it all the time, an inherent part of the commercial deal is that the script and message will not be enough to make an ad work and the stylisation of character becomes a trick to deliver a message without the viewer noticing they are being solicited. This is especially prevalent in product based commercials, where the product itself just isn't enough of a draw or has little tangible distinction. Sometimes the most elaborate animated subterfuge is undertaken to spark a flash of interest in the viewer, to effectively entertain them into submission. The other kinds of ads, the corporate branding kind, tap into a wider generic theme and use iconic association to make a mark on our minds. It's no accident that the characters in ads without physical product are the ones we enjoy and remember most at aka, they allow greater creative possibilities.

Paradoxically this is a reverse of the previous trend in animation, when characters conformed to specific styles and "cartoon" was a catch all term that established some of the world's most memorable advertising characters, tigers for petrol and cereals, etc. Though a popular way for advertisers to promote product and brand, my contention would be that more thoughtfully designed characters can do the same without necessarily feeling like advertising. A traditional "toon" character can be easily targeted to a generic group and provide alternative revenue streams through merchandising and licensing. But the same is true of more challenging design work and some characters can even live beyond their original intentions. The pugnacious knitted "Monkey" created by agency Mother for TV broadcaster "On-Digital's", is an example of a character which has achieved iconic brand status, and is still "available for work" way beyond the demise of its original sponsor.

In some way, our characters are all about subterfuge & narrative deceit. It's the application of an engaging personality to some other end than just entertainment, in this case selling product. However far you drill down looking for the art, you always have to face this truth and the trick is to keep interested enough to enjoy the game. There's many a secret to good character design, something about the eyes being too close together, the pose in silhouette, or something about the character being able to hold your gaze, but the list is as long as you want to make it. I think that "successful characterisation" depends entirely on the intended function of the idea. Character is a subjective representation, a personality acceptable through recognisably engaging narratives or a face that resonates in the mind of the viewer. There are no real secrets; there's just design that works and designs that fail. The nature of commercials is such that everything is right or appropriate at some given point, to someone somewhere. Commercial animation character design therefore constantly treads a line between an idea that is failing and a visual solution that is making it work.

What are the rules of our game?
Pictoplasma's Peter Thaler reminded me that I once said that at aka we give key importance to a graphical approach in our animation work, "finding more inspiration in clear and stylised aesthetics than in an classical Disney style". This is true, our method is less about the classical views on anatomy, pose and expression and more about the use of graphical language as a tool with which to encourage engagement with character. In other words the characters still have to appeal, in however unconventional a way we can make them. In many campaigns one is introduced to characters dependant on what the reach of the audience is guessed to be. There's a kit of parts for a character aimed at kids, and a similar set of buttons to press for more adult themed characters. But what works best is always that which plays on the opposite of what it should, dragging your interest forward and creating true unexpected presence. Sometimes the best solution to a problem is to avoid the apparent solution at all costs. If your character can kick start a sense of possibility in a brief, you sub-

sequently became bolder in your progression. In lifting your gaze from the page you can sketch into motion and dimension. The use of characters, whether employed to commercial end or as an end in themselves, is all about the marks made, be it pencil, pixel or plastic.
Our desire to find meaning comes from the commercial creative structures that exist within advertising, publishing and broadcasting. "The point" consumes everything despite the fact that much of what's made is pointless. As perpetrators we adhere to the language of branded characters as a necessary tool of our trade, but our character work can only stand out because of its distinction and diversity. It's a short tenure career for most and a long haul commitment for others. I cannot profess to offer a key diagnostic as to what denotes good design in characters, but the specific requirements of commercials – the need to present important but essentially dry visual information in an accessible and appealing way – remain the same on each and every commission. I think that's why we generally dislike working with other people's characters; you spend a disproportionate amount of time questioning why the character looks like it does and why you would have done it differently. It's no free ride working with an imported character design, and at times it's monumentally frustrating when you can't fathom them out at all. In designing bespoke characters, both in style and performance, we also look at how a unique emphasis might be given to how the essential visual information can be imparted. Sometimes its diversity is unified by colour, shape or line. In the case of nearly all our failed pitch work, it was because we had great characters that failed to

embody the message to the client. And in this subjective universe, sometimes people also just miss a good idea handed to them on a plate.

The principles of successful animated character design themselves work more by means of attrition than efficiency. Audiences used to the prevailing visual shorthand get bored and seek new styles to pigeonhole. Everything perpetually grows passé whilst originality remains the intent. It is no small irony that in our quest to create ever more diverse and surprising character forms, we create a yoke of our own devising, replacing a tiresome repetition of styles with a Sisyphean search for ever more original and unusual deign ideas. But it's addictive, once you have a reputation as a problem solver and originator, you can't stop seeking out ever more diverse solutions and pulling the rabbits from the hats. Actually it's also fun. In the era of digital media and communication, simple artistry is effectively often declared surplus to requirements; the agency process relies on statistical and focus group guidance rather than instinctive judgements. Perversely, artistry, originality and creativity have never been so in demand than now, as long as those skills can be processed with guile and whimsicality. We negotiate this path to disrupt tradition and invariably reshape the clichés where we can.
The client, agency & artist process only truly works when it results not from subjectivity and predetermination but from allied opinion and creative interaction. When this process works it defines what we like to create; the emergence of character not discernible at the outset. The messages communicated by these characters are always based on both verbal

and visual language. Various idiots have attempted to give me the precise percentages involved, but I have a clearer view that the strongest combination of these two ideals is invariably different according to circumstance, and it's always character that holds the balance. Traditional advertising (live action) refers only to communication between human beings, much of the visual shorthand is subliminal, it's part of a shared experience or moment of recognition. What's fascinating about characters in animation is that they rely heavily on these same factors to transplant us to an entirely alternate reality where we can have a relationship with quite the most bizarre creatures and still communicate effectively. This experience creates a resonant narrative and allows for brand identity to ride that narrative.

The Internet adds interesting dimensions to this. Within its nebula of text, images and sound, the Net creates a belief that the user can get in direct touch with a character that simply does not exist. This new aural and visual world gathers all this character language and visual expression into a physically limitless place and online media has developed technology of character in ways we are just now seeing in their full potential. The disposability and transient nature of much of Web character content seems to be the drifting trend at play but, whilst creative milestones stack up, we still find an eerie lack of engaging project substance from the commercial sector. The vast majority of projects of real note have been driven by self-motivation and experimentation and the Web gets used incredibly successfully as a mass communicator of homeless visual ideas and mind boggling computational experiments. Perhaps tellingly, a plethora of entrepreneurial home pages, folios and visual archives – all seeking work "off-line" in the broadcast commercial world – denote where the money's at.

Print, Broadcast, On-line or Toy line, the difficulties remain the same. Success depends on the suspension of disbelief and the authority of a character. However which way you write it, you just have to buy an animated character, in the very sense of the word. Traditional ideas of character can still be trusted close up, because their contextual value and appeal apply to any narrative. Ciphers by default only work in passing, their transience is useful and employed because nothing more is needed. Characters can make a clear demonstration of fact, theory, emotion or moment, which capitalises on the distinctiveness of the character, both from an engagement and narrative point of view, and without compromising the all-essential message. The furiously intricate motion onscreen carries what is often the key motivation behind the animation of character, that of a counterfeit elation about the underlying sales proposition, an excitement free from the restrictions of the rational and naturalistic world. In a lot of CGI animation the characters strive to look and behave almost like live action – but as Pixar's John Lassiter observes "the closer you seem to get to reality, the further away that goal appears to be." This possibly explains why the best work remains in characterisation and narrative design; it's the storytellers who interest us, and technique only comes from the creative story problem being solved. Sometimes it's a purely digital 3-D solution. At other times it's a complex array of techniques that get us where we want to go. The abandonment of conventions allows us to express more design based ethics, to emphasise colour or shape rather than squash and stretch – but not to be too reckless with tradition, as this would forget that some of those conventions are there because they really do work. Finally we can never escape the confines of a bad idea, or worse, no visible idea at all. But we can make it look great.

The assorted contents of this book will be viewed in a variety of ways; perhaps covetously and with studied curiosity, perhaps even with some subjective disdain. Those who sit desperately before life's blank sheet of paper will view it with hope, and those who find only frustration in their careers will search in paranoid hope to find, if not their own work, then those who simply marvel at the diversity of invention, intention and application on display. I am unable to claim any real authority on the subject of characterisation, but I work with it on a daily basis and I see the results of those who really know what the sum and substance of character can truly mean. Some of them are in this book.

But however delightful, everything in these pages is yesterday and tomorrow is the place to find yourself looking toward. Meanwhile, we continue working and we aim to please.

WHAT WE SEE IS LOOKING AT US

by Peter Thaler and Lars Denicke
Pictoplasma

www.pictoplasma.com

The idea for Pictoplasma came to us at the beginning of the millennium. It all started as a reaction to an overwhelming flood of iconographic figures on websites, billboards and food packaging.

We wanted to set a considered, stylistically sure-footed, high quality collection of figures against the daily glut of random mascots and pathetic sympathy seekers.

We were interested in using character design to create a memorable, up-to-date and universal language that does not have to rely on discarded, standardized clichés. And we also intended from the outset to establish a global platform, open to a whole variety of styles but above all with the guts to be stylish. A network of artists, designers and agencies came together surprisingly quickly, and now numbers 1500. Pictoplasma has developed into a lively platform, but it's a forum too. It has led to countless contacts on the scene, and thus accompanied us as we moved towards understanding character design in a completely new way.

The figures collected in our archive and those selected for this second publication show the enormous range of possibilities for achieving a high degree of recognition with fewer characteristic features. Characters are signs in an independent, graphic language. They address viewers directly, emotionally and independently of their cultural background.

And these qualities also make characters consistently important as consumption-boosting branding instruments. The best place to see how character design makes its mark on everyday life is still Tokyo. In Japan, no product, from soup to clothing to bankcards, can survive without a character, so figures and their popularity are listed and graded in a character index. This "Cuteness Hitlist" is worth millions commercially outside Asia as well, as it shows which figures' rights, and thus which licences, are most popular.

But it's not just advertising that uses figures to communicate ideas directly or to bond with the public. You can tell this by glancing at the facade of any urban building. Once they are embedded in a new context, even the cutest figures detach themselves from their original milieu, subversively conveying opinions and propaganda.

When people stopped believing in the New Media unconditionally, large numbers of unemployed graphic designers started spending time stickerbombing, posterbashing or making street art. A trained graphic designer from the glory days of advertising can't, or doesn't want to, shake off his formal language that easily. So a lot of today's Urban Art is reminiscent of Corporate Identity design. Striking logos have largely replaced the abstract "tag", often decipherable only by insiders, as a mark of recognition. Conversely, countless graffiti artists of the "old school" are shifting their visual language into three-dimensional space and designing industrially produced Urban Vinyl figurines. So while the language of brands is detaching itself from its products and circulating in public, the abstract style of a graffiti artist rediscovers itself through his or her figurine editions on the shelves of global toy chains. Like any living language, the language of character design is changing as well. It is adapting to current trends in art, politics and current events. It is taking up existing aesthetic concepts, then remixing and sampling them, combining meanings and formulations, creating new sensory connections and varying the context.

When Pictoplasma was launched as an on-line project in 2000, it was closely linked with this medium. The computer, the Internet and the screen surface served as both tool and medium. They provided a grid, and a technique for creating characters as pixels or vectors, logos or 3-D figures. The ever-increasing possibilities available were a constant spur to implement designs more and more expressively, three-dimensionally and memorably, but they still ended up on one surface only – a screen or a printed page. The reduced and perfect figures produced in this way were always symptoms of lost physical reality as well – or at least the partly hysterical discourse that propagated such loss as part of hyperreality saw them as such. Every highlight on the smooth surface reinforced this feeling of loss.

There are countless examples to prove how artists and designers became increasingly less willing to settle for simply producing perfect, shallow, sterile illustrations. Character design has liberated itself from the conditions imposed by a market economy with a target audience made up of minors, and is increasingly prepared to risk leaping into the third dimension. The longing for actual physical quality is driving designers the world over to the sewing machine, so that they can actually take one of their creatures in their arms. And this does not produce teddy bears, but consistent character design.

Pictoplasma 2 aims to show the surprising abundance of resources and styles that are now deployed to create recognition values with characters, and additionally concentrates on their actual use – whether as merchandising products, in advertising campaigns, on building facades or in galleries, as graphics, figurines or rag dolls. The important thing here is not whether you screw a robot together from wood, mould it from plastic, assemble it from recyclable polystyrene waste or cast it in precious metal. Even a graphic revision of the ground plan of a Romanesque church can summon up gigantic androids before our eyes.

True quality remains the skilfully executed, strong visual idea, and the figure's ability to reach the viewer.

EDITORIAL   INDEX

by Robert Klanten
Die Gestalten Verlag

This book is the distillation of the over 8500 works of art that we were sent. That's 290 CD-ROMs worth of material. Given that amount, each chapter could have been made into an entire book. That's why this book does not claim to be a complete record of current character design. Rather, it is a very systematic selection that developed over nine months in accordance with multiple editorial considerations. Without Pictoplasma 1 we could have certainly weighed the selection shown here differently, but we didn't think it made sense to simply repeat a successful formula. Instead of going that route, we sought to establish a relationship to Pictoplasma 1 by incorporating the experiences we had with that book as well as current developments in design into this book in a consequential way. That explains why the strong tendency to take characters from the second to the third dimension that has developed over the last few years is given ample space in two chapters about puppets, action figures and figurative objects. In this work the separation between character design and art becomes increasingly blurry. We have included these examples intentionally in order to reflect the current dispute between art and aspects of the depiction of figures or their human traits. The chapter "Pixel" is no longer included in this book although the design direction has become very popular. In our opinion, this popularity has strangled most of the potential of the pixel aesthetic. In fact, most of the work we saw seemed to us to be copies of well-known approaches by established protagonists. Some work that was above this suspicion can be found in the chapter "Vector". When it came to freehand drawings, we found that a disposition toward illustration

dominated much of the work that we received. We decided to concentrate on artwork that represented a fresh take on character design instead. Today, characters appear on various stages as vectors, graphics or 3-D renderings, as action figures, puppets, children's toys, etc. They are perhaps becoming most present in the area of urban art, the modern variety of graffiti that disrupts, comments on and reflects cityscapes through drawn, spray-painted or pasted-on figures. The recognition value of characters not only establishes an identity for their creators, but it also attracts mostly positive attention from observers in our overloaded cityscapes. In many cases, we could have presented all of the different applications of various techniques and materials together for purposes of comparison. But because we didn't think that would be a very exciting approach to character design, we have mostly featured only one example in each relevant chapter. We felt it would be more interesting to show how variations on a theme could be created with a single canon of forms. That's why Pictoplasma 2 features multiple "families" – thematically similar characters done by one artist. Sometimes only a "hairstyle" or "clothing" is changed, often the "anatomy" varies, but the relationships of the figures to each other and the signature of the artist remain clearly visible. As before, vector graphics still make up the majority of the works presented. What's noticeable is the uninhibited way that computers are being used to create compositions that look like they've been cut out with scissors or psychedelic collages. These artworks have expanded the stylistic repertoire of vector graphics.

You should bear in mind that many of the characters are more than just random designs in most of the works shown across the chapters here. They are their designers' little trademarks, and they stick in our memories. It doesn't matter if they're exploited commercially or simply function as signs or sympathy seekers, in many cases a great deal of effort has gone into creating them. And for this reason alone the designers responsible would certainly be pleased to have some feedback.

VECTOR

When people started drawing characters with vector graphics, they used compasses, ruler and stencil to make their characters plannable and repeatable. Today the computer programmes' toolboxes have honed this task to perfection. The modern viewer has much better visual training and is able to "read" very simple or complicated geometric shapes, to test them for various visual standards and to assign specific information to them on different interpretational levels. The formal abstraction and simplification of colour schemes or the readability of very small sizes at long distances has been developed to fulfil industrial demands and has been cultivated by the viewer. Characters generated through vector graphics are ideally suited for a context dominated by similar design shapes and techniques or situations generated by similar computer programmes. That's why they are often found together with vector graphics and typography as well as with consumer and goods aesthetics.

The works shown here are a further development: an analogue design approach like traditional silhouettes or collages is being revived. Many designers also make a deliberate attempt to strip the artificial "smoothness" off computer-generated images, or conversely to reinforce this further, thus making it seem even more artificial. The austere, technically-inspired use as a black-and-white picto or logo is frequently distorted by the figure's very bizarre design. 3-D rendering versions have become even more popular and are often a preliminary step towards an action figure.

01

02   03

04   05

01 Manu Burghart | 02-04 Grace Montemar | 05 Meomi Design

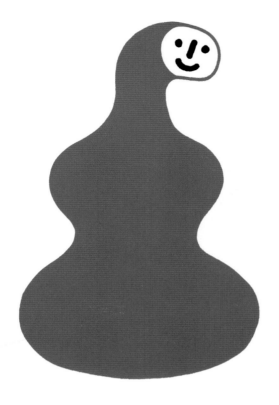

01

02

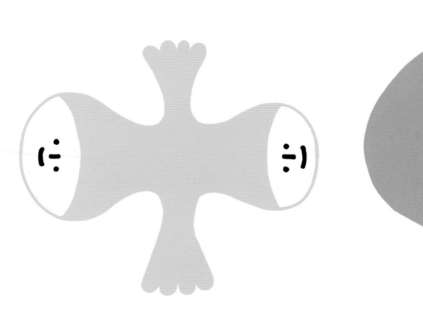

03

04

01-04 Aki

01

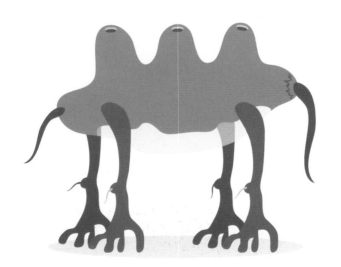

02

03

01-03 Haraldur Agnar Civelek

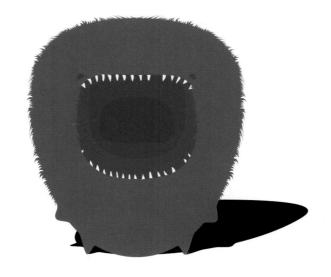

01

02

03

04

01-04 FriendsWithYou

01   02   03   04   05

06   07   08   09   10

11   12   13   14   15

16   17   18   19   20

21   22   23   24   25

01-25 FriendsWithYou

01

02

03

04

01-04 FriendsWithYou

01 Unit9 | 02-04 Dennis Worden | 05 Sektie | 06 Allan Sanders | 07 Tim Biskup

01-04 Fleecircus

01 02 03 04 05 06
07 08 09 10 11 12
13 14 15 16 17 18
19 20 21 22 23 24
25 26 27 28 29 30
31 32 33 34

01 02 03 04

05 06 07 08

09 10 11 12

13 14 15 16

01-16 Mori Chack / Pony Canyon

01

02

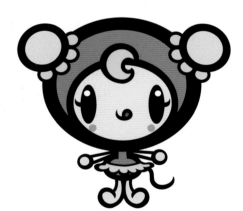

03

04

05

06

07

08

01-02 Hideyuki Tanaka | 03-08 Ayumi Mori

01

02   03   04   05

01 Syrup | 02-05 Mark Rigney

01

02

03

04

05

06

07

08

09

01 Junko Mizuno | 02-03 Raoul Deleo | 04-06 Incorect | 07-09 Maria Pia

01

02   03   04

01-04 Misery

01   02   03   04   05   06

07   08   09   10   11   12

13   14   15   16   17   18

19   20   21   22   23   24

25   26   27   28   29   30

31   32   33   34   35   36

01-06 Digart Graphics | 07-12 Attaboy | 13-16 Itsuo Ito | 19-24 Digart Graphics
25-33 James Lassey | 34-36 Mari-chan

01   02   03   04   05

06   07   08   09   10

11   12   13   14   15

16   17   18   19   20

21   22   23   24   25

01-25 Mari-chan

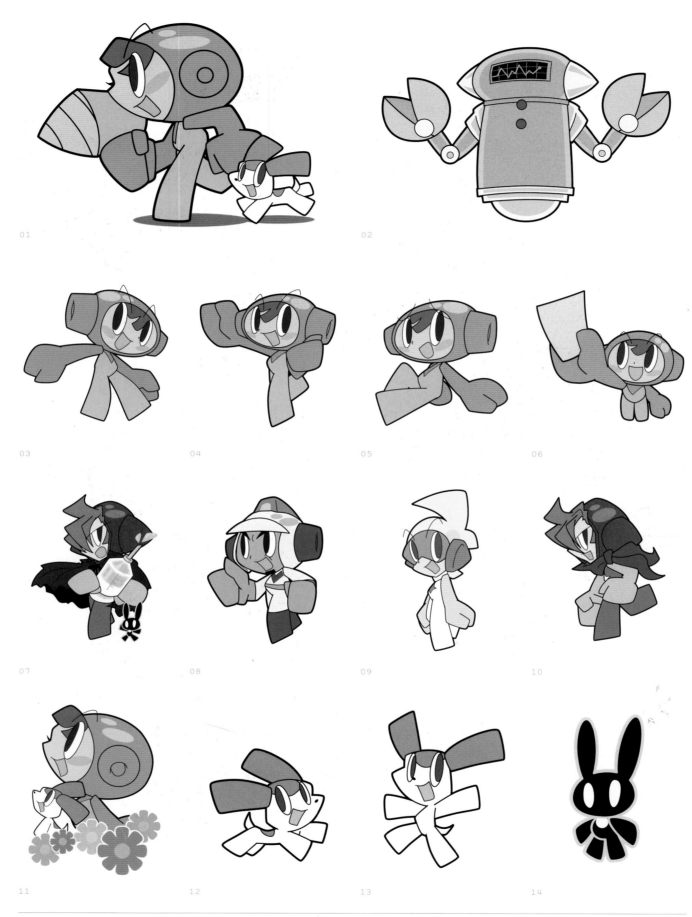

01

02

03

04

05

06

07

08

09

10

11

12

13

14

01   02   03   04   05   06

07   08   09   10   11   12

13   14   15   16   17   18

19   20   21   22   23   24

25   26   27   28   29   30

31   32   33   34   35   36

01-18 Satoshi Matsuzawa | 19-26 Unit9 | 27-29 Itsuo Ito | 30 Raoul Deleo | 31-35 Unit9
36 Hideyuki Tanaka

01   02   03   04   05   06

07   08   09   10   11

12   13   14   15   16   17

18   19   20   21   22   23

24   25   26   27   28   29

30   31   32   33   34   35

01-17 Unit9 | 18-23 Michael Salter | 24-35 Moti

01

02

03

04

05

06

07

08

09

10

01-02 Genevieve Gauckler | 03-10 Jimba

01

02

03

01-03 Büro Destruct

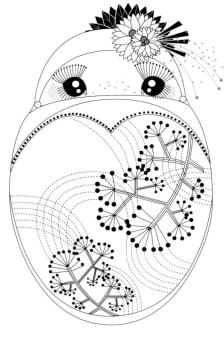

01

02

01

02

03

04

01-04 Unit9

01   02   03

04   05   06   07   08   09

10   11   12   13   14   15

16   17   18   19   20   21

22   23   24   25   26   27

01-15 Gastòn Caba | 16-18 Benjamin von Eckartsberg | 19-21 Cubemen | 22-25 Sanjai Bhana
26-27 Cubemen

Katherine Aoki

01-03 Starstyling | 04 Benwar Home Design

James Marshall / Dalek

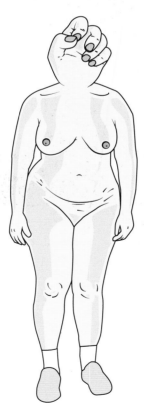

01-02 Unit9 | 03-04 Incorect

01-02 Phunk

01 Danny Merk | 02 Christoph Hoppenbrock

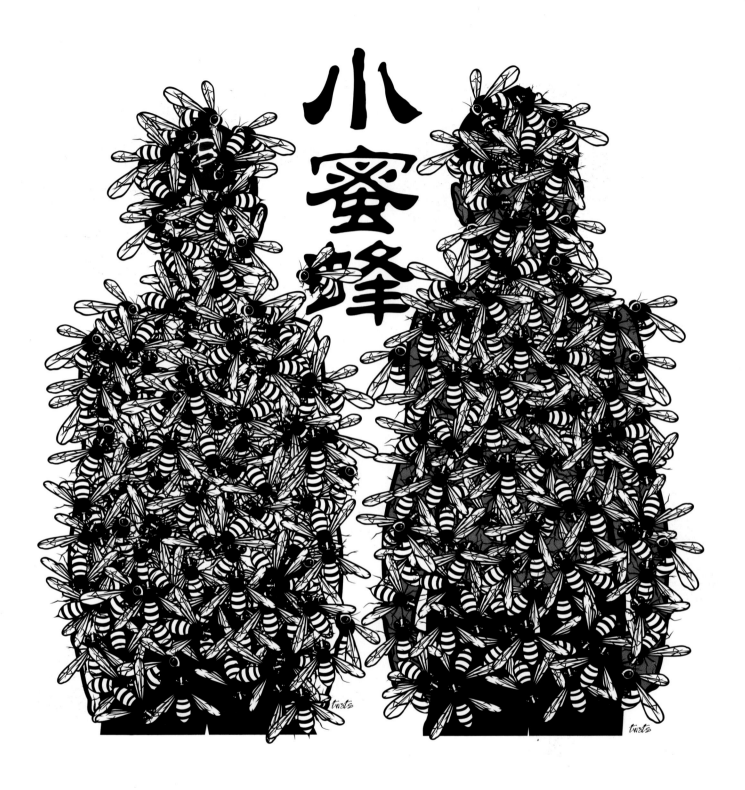

Phunk

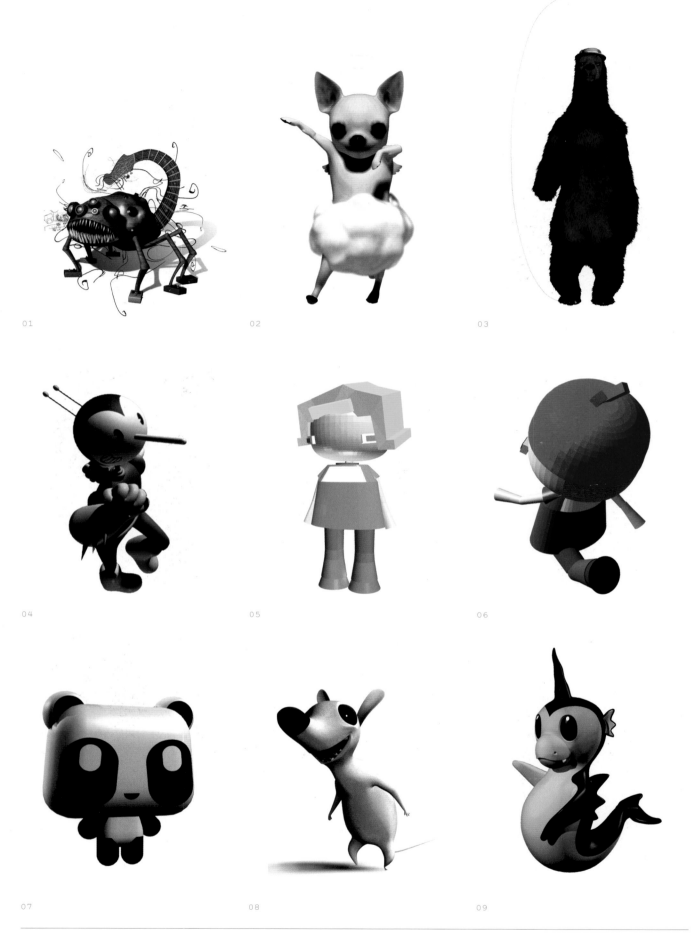

01   02   03

04   05   06

07   08   09

01 Paco Aguayo | 02 Junya Nishioka / Tex Agency | 03 Studio Soi / Stenner & Schuh | 04 Benwar
Home Design | 05-06 Futurefarmers | 07 Superdeux | 08 Studio Soi / Unseld & Schuh | 09 Com Com

01   02   03

04   05   06

07   08   09

01–06 Klaus Haapaniemi | 07–09 Arlo Johns

01

02

03

04

05

06

07

08

09

10

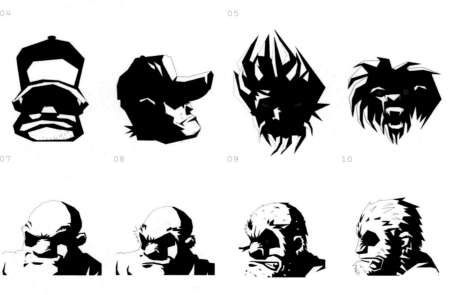

11

12

13

14

15

01-15 Unit9

01

02

03

04

01 Daniel Althausen | 02-03 Shroomboy | 04 Daniel Althausen

01

02

03

04

05

01-05 Gama-Go

01

02   03   04   05   06   07

01-07 Gama-Go

01

02

03

04

01 Allan Sanders | 02 Tim Biskup | 03 Allan Sanders | 04 Frédérique Bertrand

01

02

03

04

01-04 Frédérique Bertrand

01

02

03

04

01 Paula Castro Tizado | 02 Evil Cuppycake | 03-04 Paula Castro Tizado

01

02

03

04

01-04 Manu Burghart

01

02

03

04

05

06

07

08

09

10

11

01–08 Junko Mizuno | 09–11 Emma

01

02 03 04 05

06 07 08 09

01-09 Marie Caillou

01

02　　　　　　　　03　　　　　　　　04

01–04 Marie Caillou

Fawn Gehweiler

Fawn Gehweiler

01–04 Miss Van

Miss Van

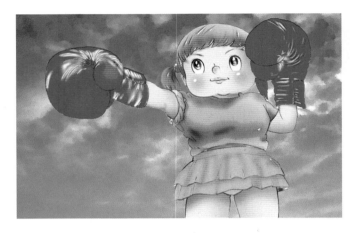

01

02

03

04

01-02 Katsuki Tanaka | 03-04 Misery

01

02

03

01-03 Sebastiaan Van Doninck

Christian Montenegro

Christian Montenegro

Christian Montenegro

01

02   03   04   05   06   07

01-07 Christian Montenegro

01

02

03

04

01-04 Jimba

01

02

03

04

01-04 Julia Schonlau

01

02

03

04

05

06

07

08

09

10

11

12

13

14

15

16

17

18

19

20

01 Benwar Home Design | 02 Jum | 03-20 Keiichi Bandou

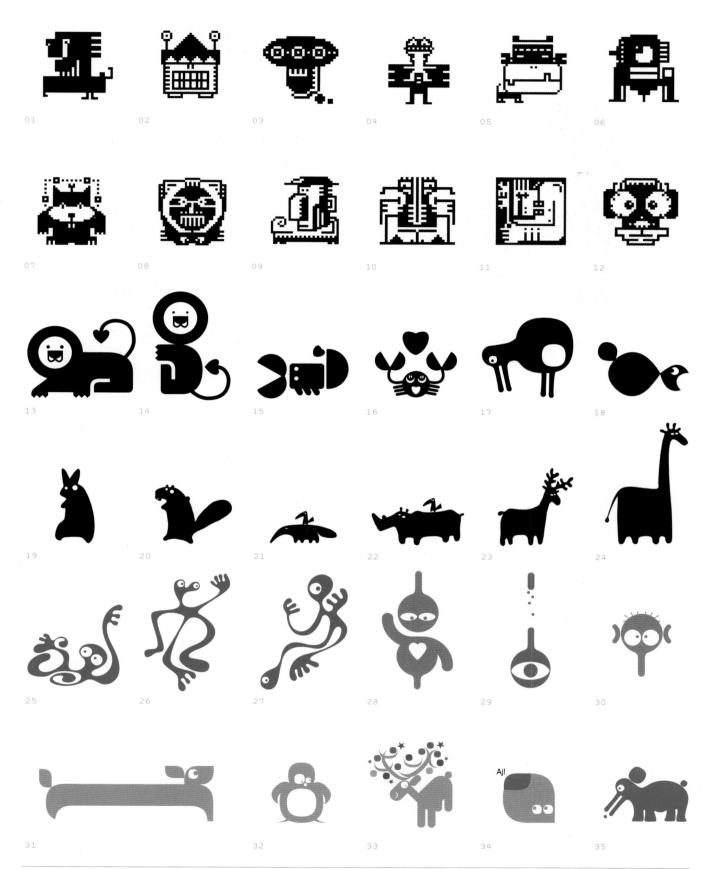

01   02   03   04   05   06

07   08   09   10   11   12

13   14   15   16   17   18

19   20   21   22   23   24

25   26   27   28   29   30

31   32   33   34   35

01-12 Benwar Home Design | 13-16 Jakob Kanior | 17-18 Genevieve Gauckler | 19-24 Airside
25-35 Genevieve Gauckler

01 02 03 04 05 06

07 08 09 10 11 12

13 14 15 16 17 18

19 20 21 22 23

24 25 26 27 28 29

30 31 32 33 34 35

01-35 Genevieve Gauckler

01

02

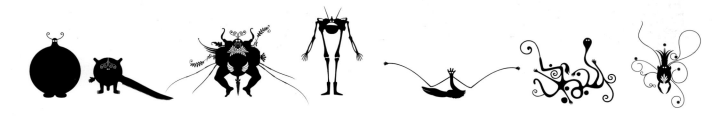

03

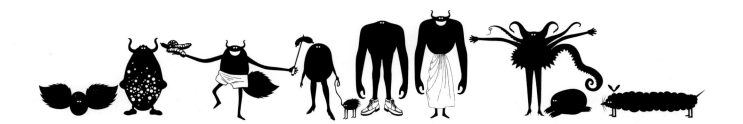

04

01-04 Genevieve Gauckler

01

01-02 Genevieve Gauckler

Genevieve Gauckler

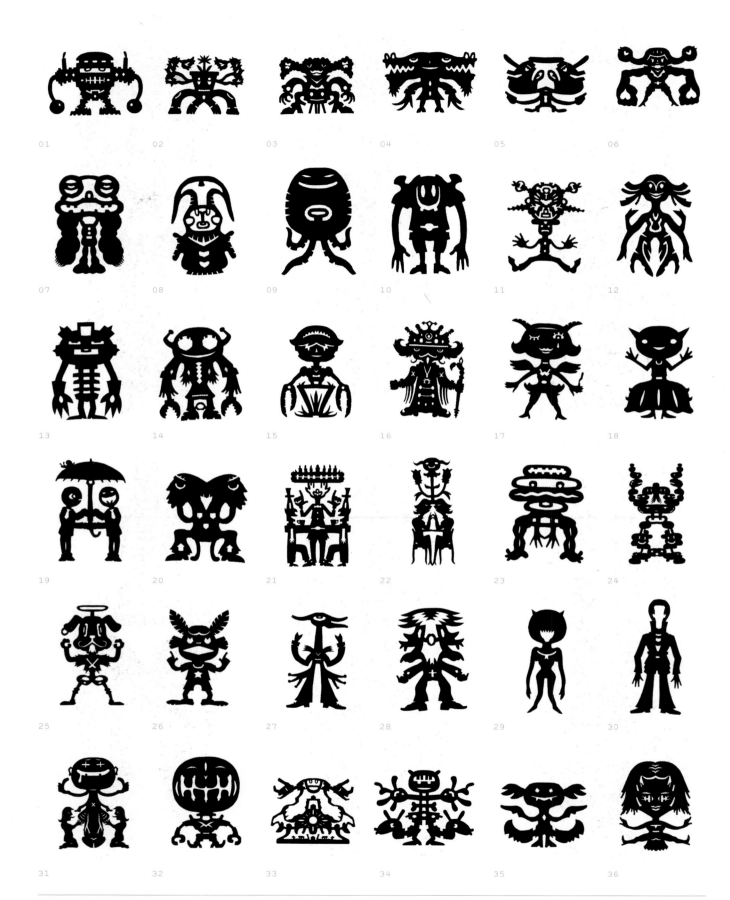

01 02 03 04 05 06

07 08 09 10 11 12

13 14 15 16 17 18

19 20 21 22 23 24

25 26 27 28 29 30

31 32 33 34 35 36

01—36 Ryohei Tanaka

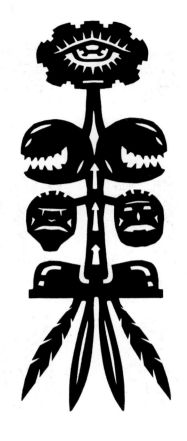

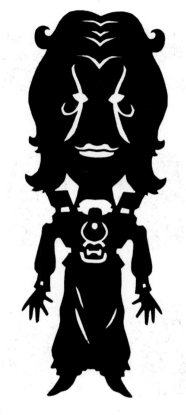

01

02

03

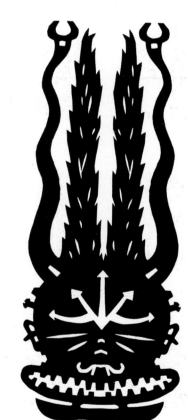

04

05

06

01-06 Ryohei Tanaka

Ryohei Tanaka

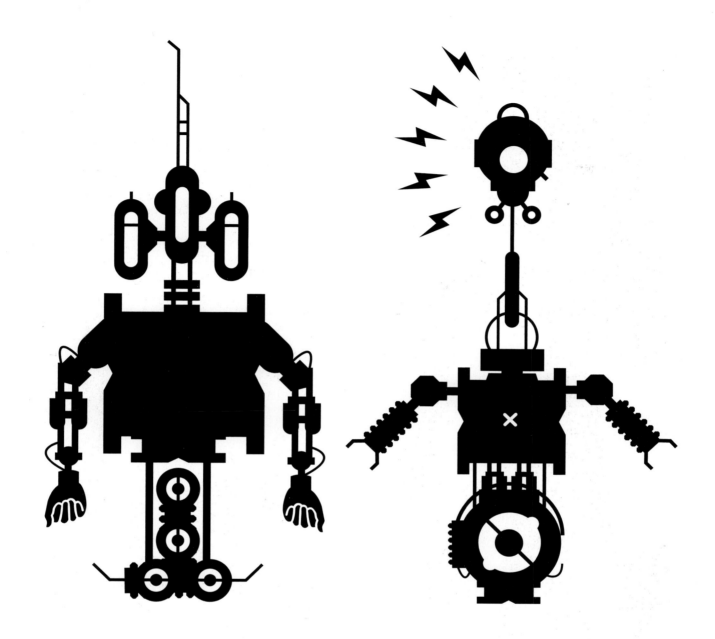

Incorect

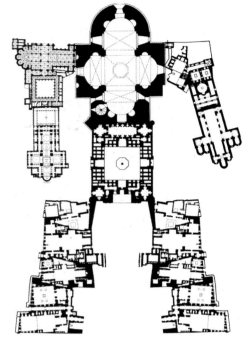

01

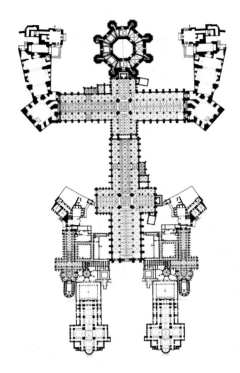

02

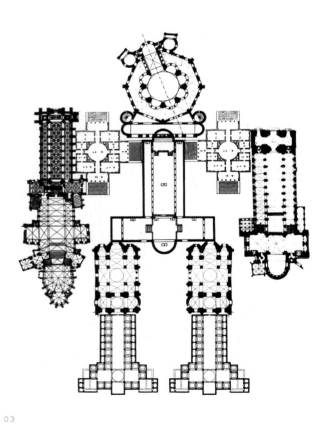

03

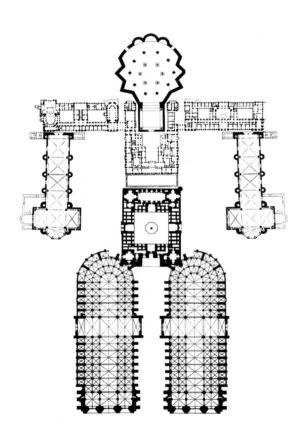

04

01–04 Peter Rentz

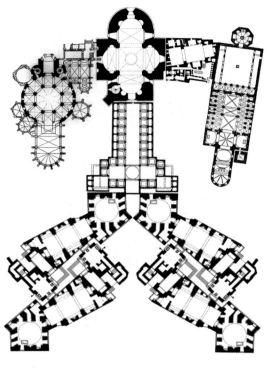

01

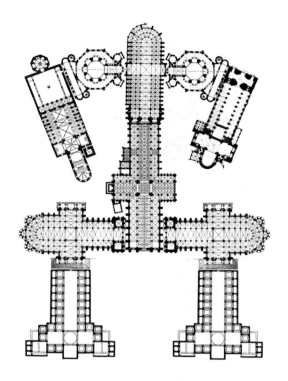

02

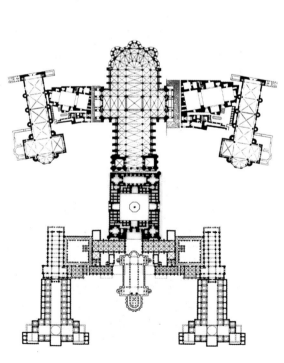

03

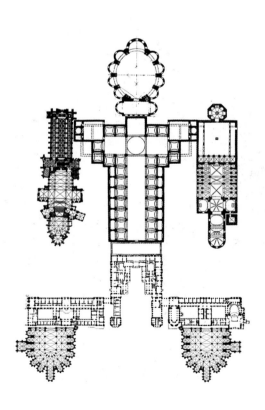

04

01–04 Peter Rentz

01

02

03

04

01-04 Genevieve Gauckler

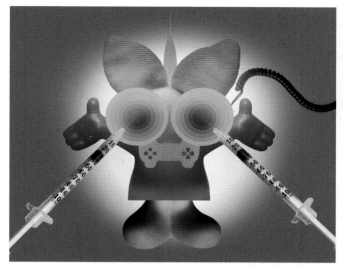

01

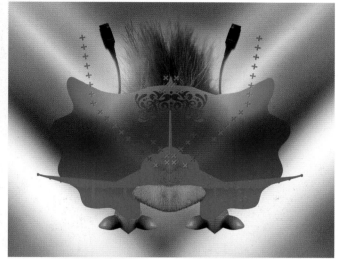

02

03

04

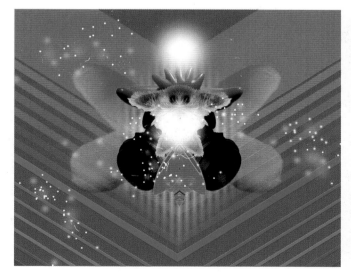

05

06

01–06 Genevieve Gauckler

01

02

03

04

01-04 Genevieve Gauckler

Christian Montenegro

Klaus Haapaniemi

01

03

04

05

06

07

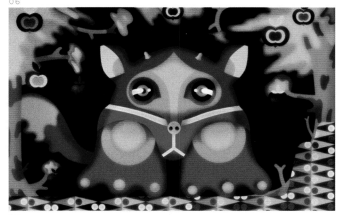

08

01-08 Klaus Haapaniemi

01

02

03

04

05

06

07

08

01-08 Klaus Haapaniemi

01

02

01-02 Klaus Haapaniemi

01

02

03

04

05

06

01-06 Klaus Haapaniemi

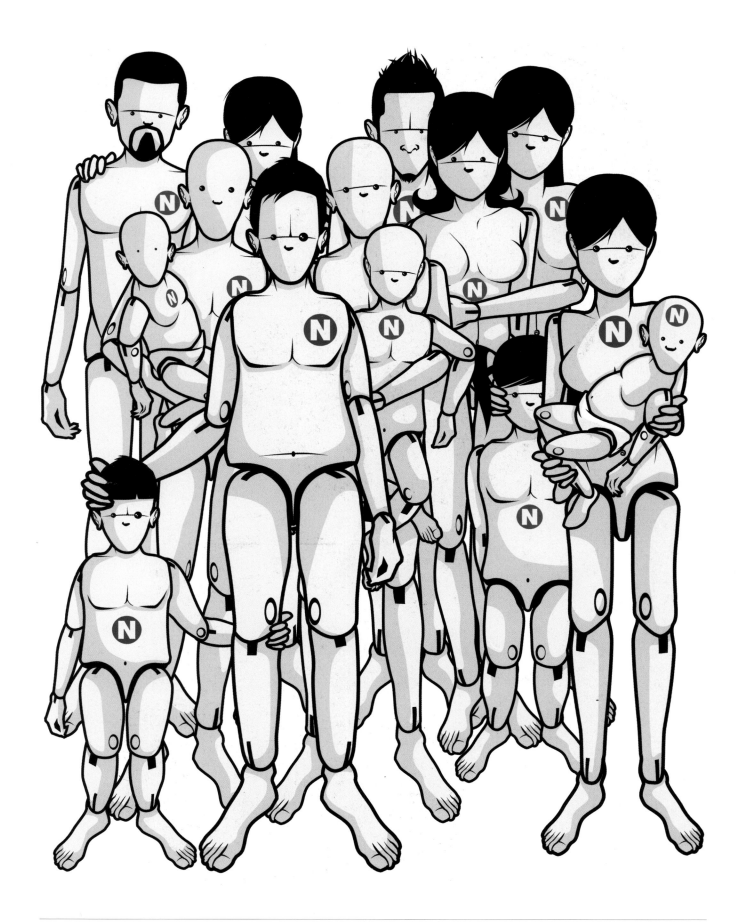

Phunk

01

02

03

04

01-04 Tadashi Gozu

Tadashi Gozu

01　　　　　　　　　02　　　　　　　　　03

04　　　　05　　　　06　　　　07　　　　08　　　　09

10　　　　11　　　　12　　　　13　　　　14　　　　15

16　　　　17　　　　18　　　　19　　　　20　　　　21

22　　　　23　　　　24　　　　25　　　　26　　　　27

01-27 Nanospore

01-27 Cubemen

01   02   03   04   05

06   07   08   09   10

11   12   13   14   15

16   17   18   19   20

21   22   23   24   25

01-25 Unit9

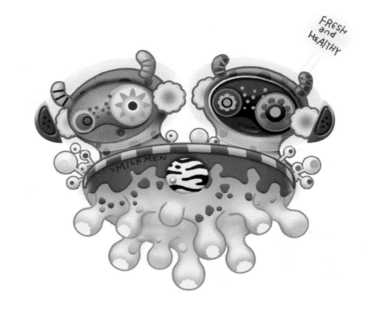

01

02

03

04

05

06

07

08

09

10

11

12

13

14

15

16

17

01-17 D'Holbachie-Yoko

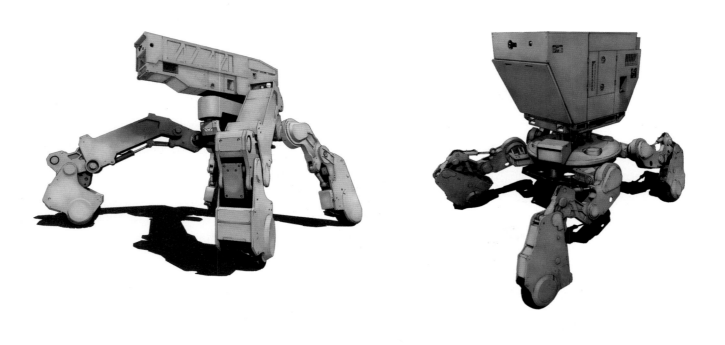

01   02

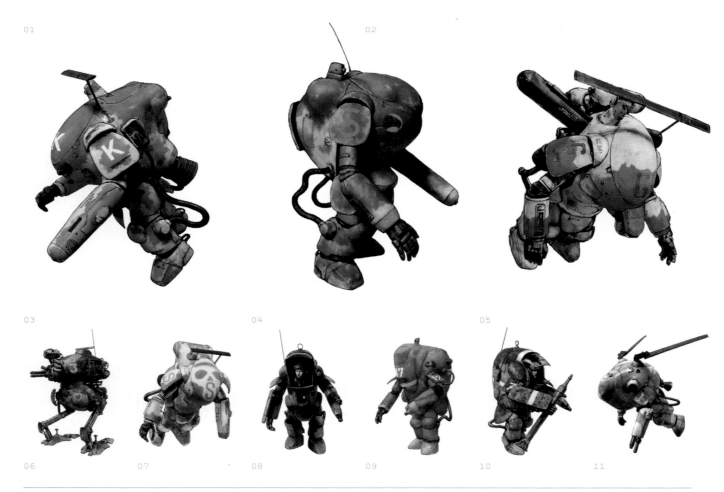

03   04   05

06   07   08   09   10   11

01-02 Junji Okubo / Izmo Juki | 03-11 Kow Yokoyama

Tokyoplastic

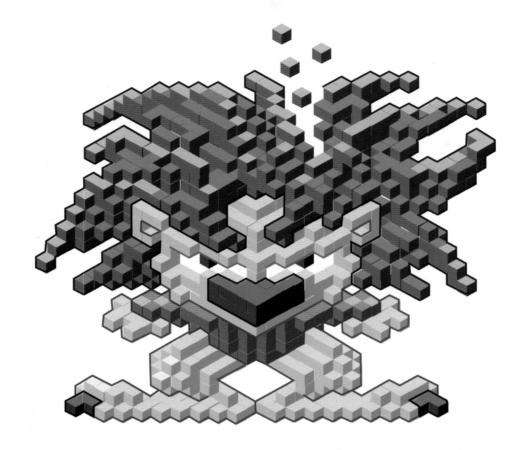

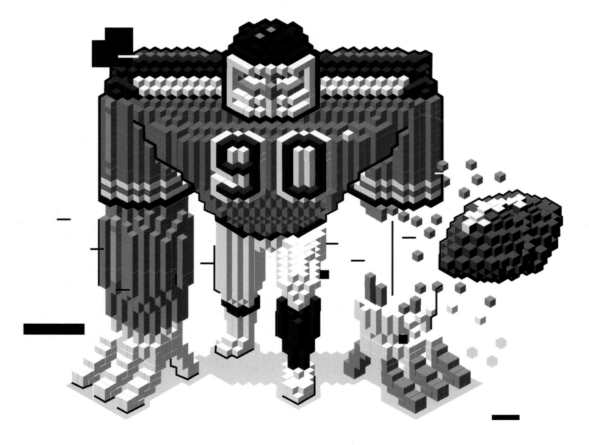

01-02 Raoul Deleo

01   02   03

04   05   06

07   08   09

2

ACTION FIGURES

Action figures are collectibles, in other words toys for adults. While puppets and dolls are "high touch", the little vinyl figures represent "high tech". They are precise, clean, usually slick and painted, destined for the home showcase and really more a "boys' thing". The point is simply to own them, they are a material version of something that has so far tended to be virtual, and have no practical use value. Originally action figures come from the world of cartoons and were traditionally sold in comic shops. Soon science fiction and fantasy figures came along, and nowadays you can buy religious or political action figures as well. Action figures are most important in Japan, Korea and the USA. The action figures shown here are all so-called designer toys. They are often three-dimensional versions of well-known designs or illustrations, which are then sold as short series. But unlike the traditional figures the designer toys are not merchandise from a familiar comic series, a TV format or a feature film. The action figures shown here are not subject to the constraints of illustrating an introduced format precisely. They celebrate themselves and thus their creators as well, who often enjoy cult status through them.

As designer toys are not tied to existing models, their designers consistently take liberties. Often the figures are bizarre, politically incorrect, tend to have a rough appearance and are definitely not Disney's idea of a leading man.

Tofer

01 02 03 04

05 06 07 08

09 10 11 12

13 14 15 16

01–16 Anchovy, 2000

01   02   03

04   05   06   07

08   09   10

11   12   13

01-03 © Namaiki | 04-07 Michael Salter | 08-10 Yoshimoto Kogyo Co., Ltd. / Maywa Denki
11-13 Devilrobots

01

02

03

04

05

06

07

08

09

10

01 Devilrobots | 02 David Choe | 03-06 Bufalo Club | 07-09 Nathan Jurevicius
10 Devilrobots / © Evirob

01

02

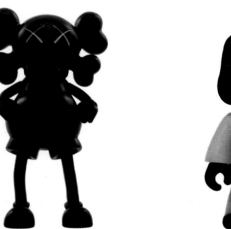

03

04

05

01-02 Critterbox Toys / Dave Cooper | 03 Kaws | 04 Ewos | 05 Rolito / Toy2R

01

02

03   04   05   06

07   08   09   10

01-10 Picopico

Junko Mizuno

01

02

03

04

01-04 Junko Mizuno

01   02   03   04   05

06   07   08   09   10

11   12   13   14   15

16   17   18   19   20

21   22   23   24   25

Sony Creative Products Inc. | 01-05 © Moto Hideyasu | 06-10 © 2003 Winney Co.
11-15 © Ado Mizumori | 16-20 © 2003 Pete Fowler | 21-25 © Delta Inc.

01   02   03

01   02   03

Mood
RAT

01

02

03

04

05

06

Sony Creative Products Inc. | 01-06 © Fafi 2003

01

02

07

08

09

Sony Creative Products Inc. | 01-06 Madreal Derrick Hodgson

01

02

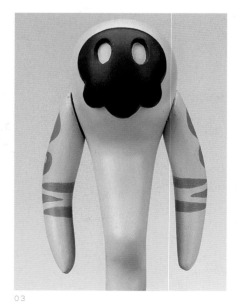

03

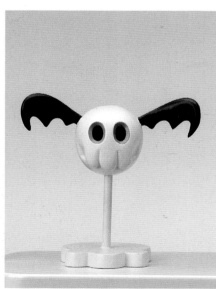

04

05

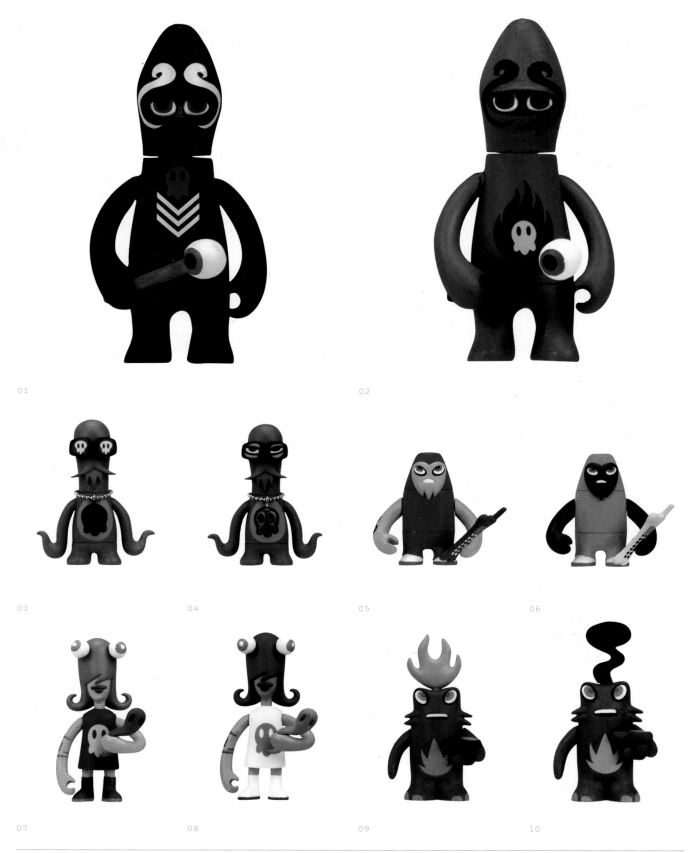

01

02

03

04

05

06

07

08

09

10

01

02

03

04

05

01

02

03

04

05

06

01-06 Furi Furi Company

01

03

02

04

Coarsetoys / Germany

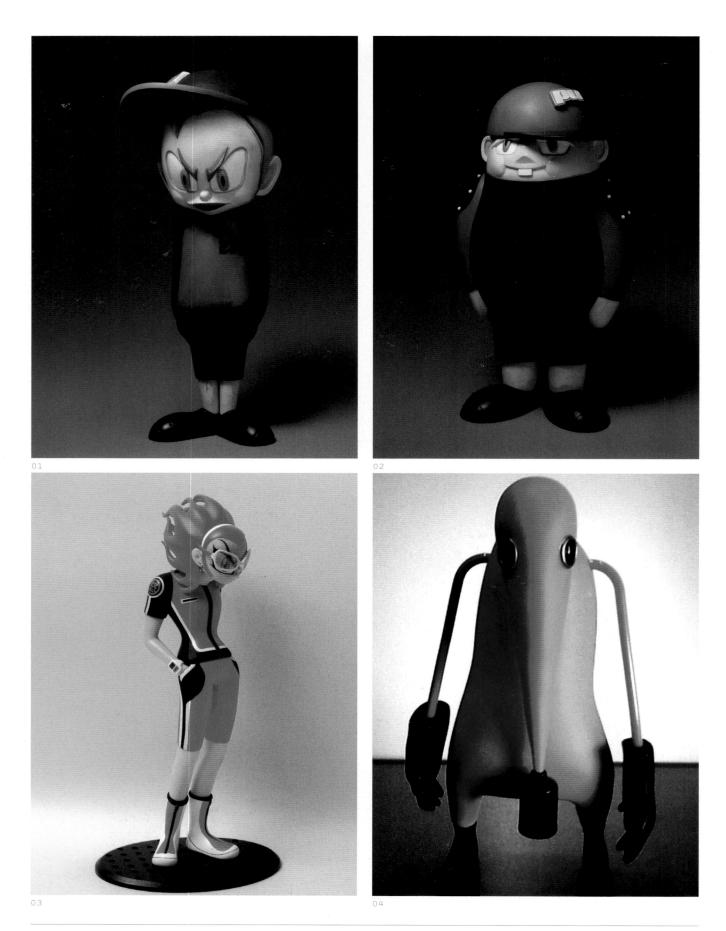

01

02

03

04

01-03 Koji Takeuchi a.k.a. Astro Graphica | 04 Tokion / Os Gemeos

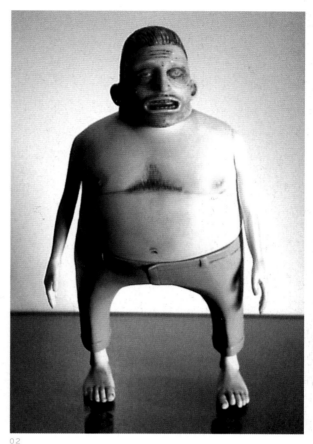

01

02

03

04

01 Tokion / Margaret Kilgallen | 02 Tokion / Barry McGee (Twist)
03 Tokion / Shepard Fairey (Obey Giant) | 04 Tokion / Stash

01

02

01-02 Yukinori Dehara

Mamiko Hasebe

Paul McCarthy

01

02

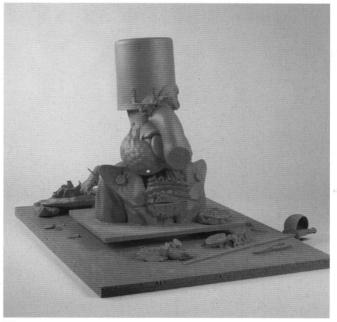

03

01-03 Paul McCarthy

PUPPETS, DOLLS & OBJECTS

Puppets and dolls are "high touch", cuddly, warm, more interactive and more social than the somewhat aloof action figures. They sit on the sofa at home and keep the man of the house company. They are clearly undergoing something of a boom and there are various reasons for this. For one thing, puppets and dolls were something we related to as children, and now we do it as adults. Rediscovering them and admitting they're cute probably comes from Japan, where character and child traditionally enter into longer and more intensive relationships because of the day school system. The Manga/Anime genre brought the young comic world and adult pop culture together. The puppets and dolls shown here are often linked with adult themes (boxing, Ku-Klux-Klan, S&M), and translating these into children's toys is a playful way of adapting and processing the adult world (catharsis). These incorrect puppets and dolls create friction with the viewer and thus strike up a personal contact as well. But it is also striking that the often rustic implementation makes them seem clumsy, they deliberately try to look homemade and so appear to be more personal than mass produced goods, even when they are bought as presents.

The puppet and doll boom is also inspired by the fact that there is now a generation of parents who are used to setting themselves up very stylishly and to surrounding themselves with appropriate objects. This generation of very knowing purchasers cannot identify with mainstream children's products of the kind offered by department store toy sections, and they don't want to be identified with them when giving presents to parents and children.

01

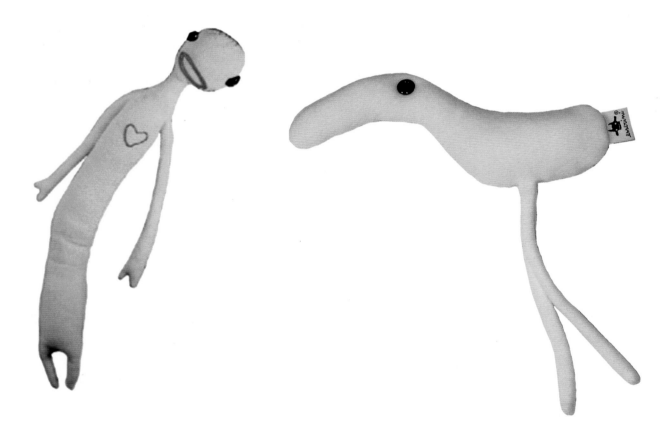

02
03

01-03 Esserini

01 02 03

04 05 06

07 08 09

01-03 Crashcarcity | 04-08 © Cube Co.,Ltd. / Ayumi Urayama | 09 Mari-chan

01

02 03 04

01-04 Hoboyard Toy Co.

01

02

03

04

05

06

01-06 Rinzen

01

02

03

04

05

06

07

08

09

10

01–10 FriendsWithYou

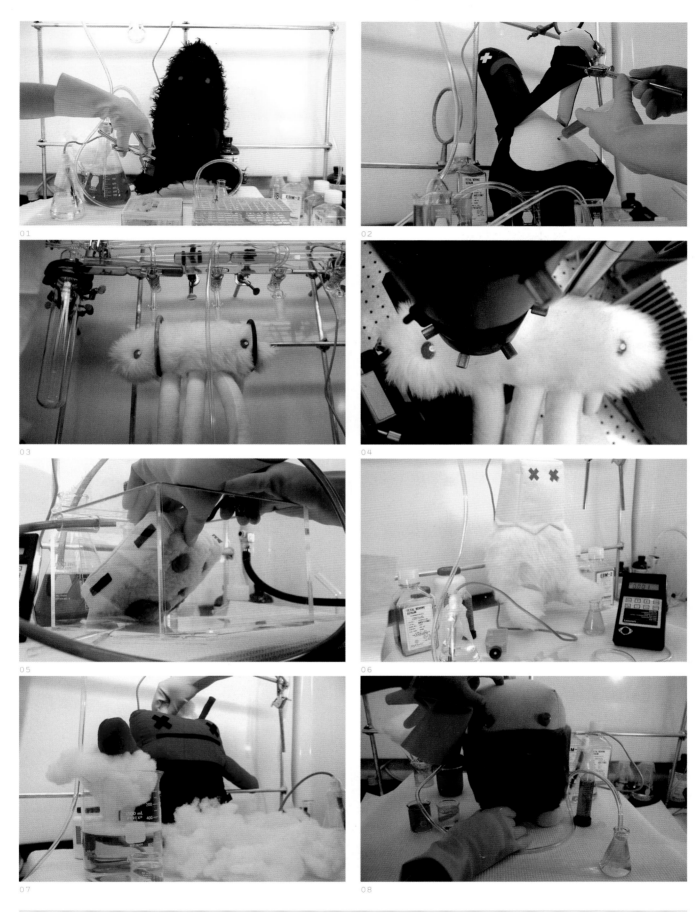

01

02

03

04

05

06

07

08

01-08 FriendsWithYou

01   02   03   04

05   06   07   08

09   10   11   12

13   14   15   16

01–16 Boris Hoppek

140

01

02

03

01 Boris Hoppek | 02 YiYing Wang | 03 Boris Hoppek

01 02 03 04 05 06
07 08 09 10 11 12
13 14 15 16 17 18
19 20 21 22 23 24
25 26 27 28 29 30
31 32 33 34 35 36

01-36 Mumbleboy

01   02   03   04

05   06   07   08

09   10   11   12

13   14   15   16

01-02 Cosmic Debris | 03-04 Silas Hickey and Tsuka | 5-6 Marimo Craft / Hory's | 07 Tsai-Fi
08 Picopico | 09 Airside | 10 Tado | 11 Gaga Inc | 12 Silas Hickey and Tsuka | 13 Gaga Inc
14 Crashcarcity | 15 Silas Hickey and Tsuka | 16 Crashcarcity

01 Sofuzzycrew | 02-03 Grace Montemar

01

02

03

04

01-04 Love Ablan

01 02 03 04 05 06 07

01-02 Meomi Design | 03-06 Georgie & Timmy | 07 Gastón Pérsico

01 Gaga Inc | 02 Aranzi Aronzo | 03-04 Gaga Inc | 05 Sanrio Company, Ltd. | 06 Gwen Yip
07-09 Marion Rutz-Kaschtalinski

01

02

03

04

05

01

02

03

04

01-02 Mari-chan | 03-04 Cosmic Debris / Brian Charles Brooks

01

02

01-02 Little Miss Luzifer™

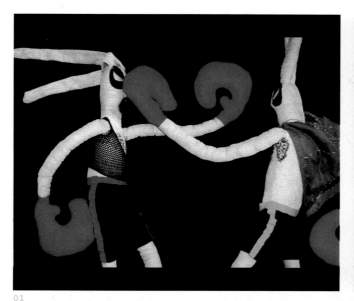

01

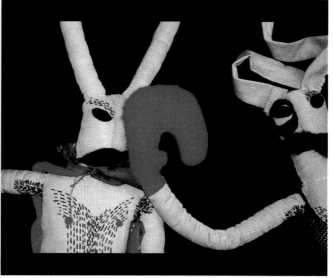

02

03

04

01-02 Rina Donnersmarck | 03-04 Tender Fury

Mari-chan

01-02 Mari-chan | 03-04 Büro Destruct | 05-06 Devilrobots

Juan Pablo Cambariere

154

01   02

03   04

01-04 Juan Pablo Cambariere

01

02

03

04

05

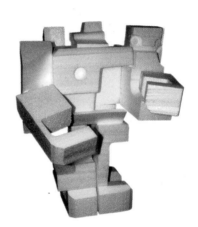

06

07

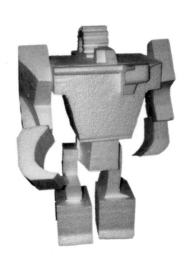

08

09

01-09 Michael Salter

Michael Salter

01

02

03

01-03 Eliezer Sonnenschien

Eliezer Sonnenschien

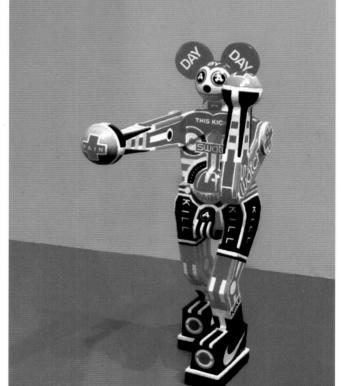

01-03 Eliezer Sonnenschien

01

02   03

01-03 Eliezer Sonnenschien

01

02

03

04

01

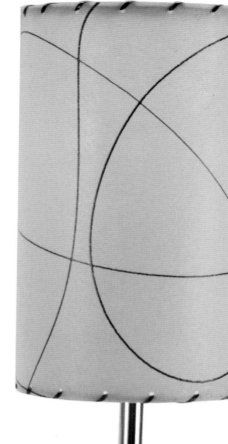

02

03

01–03 Shag

4

FREEHAND DRAWING

In this chapter the hand-held drawing implement acts as a starting point and means of expression in character design. The movements of hand and arm are translated directly via the selected drawing medium as well as the pressure and angle on the blotting pad. Freehand drawing is therefore predestined to capture the spontaneous personal mood and to create imperfect and thus particularly expressive, alive characters. The huge variety of drawing media and the way they are used invariably lead to the artist's injecting personal expression and style.

At present there seems to be a tendency towards the one-liner in character design: form is defined by a single line, often drawn without taking the pencil off the paper (as in the children's house-drawing game). But it is striking that using computers to design figures has become increasingly popular recently. Freehand drawing is used particularly when its specific expression is desirable. The incomplete, rough element is transferred directly into the figures, which makes them look rough and threatening. The selections made for the chapter entirely reflect the range of works submitted.

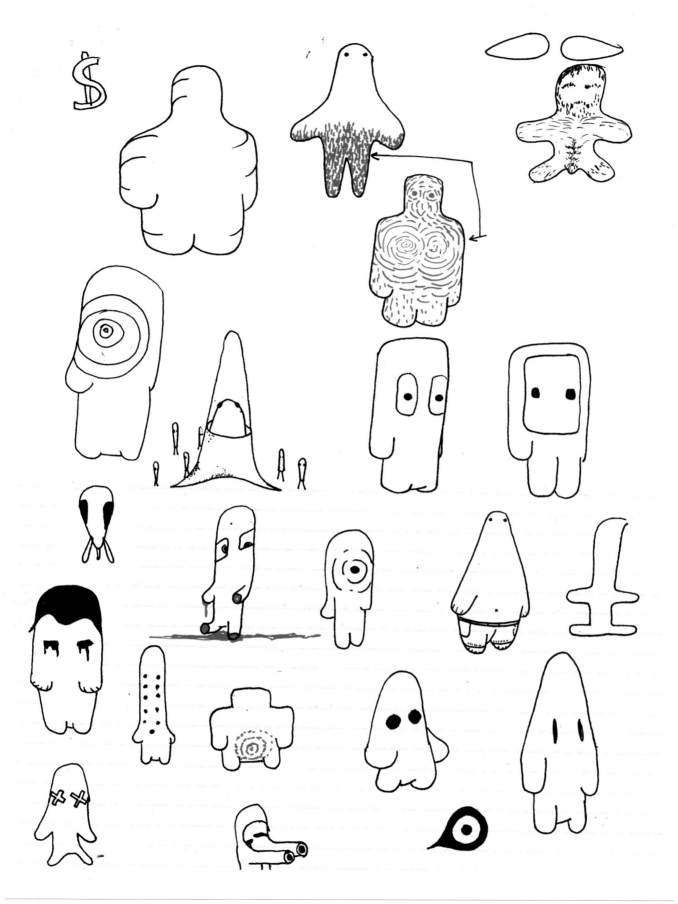

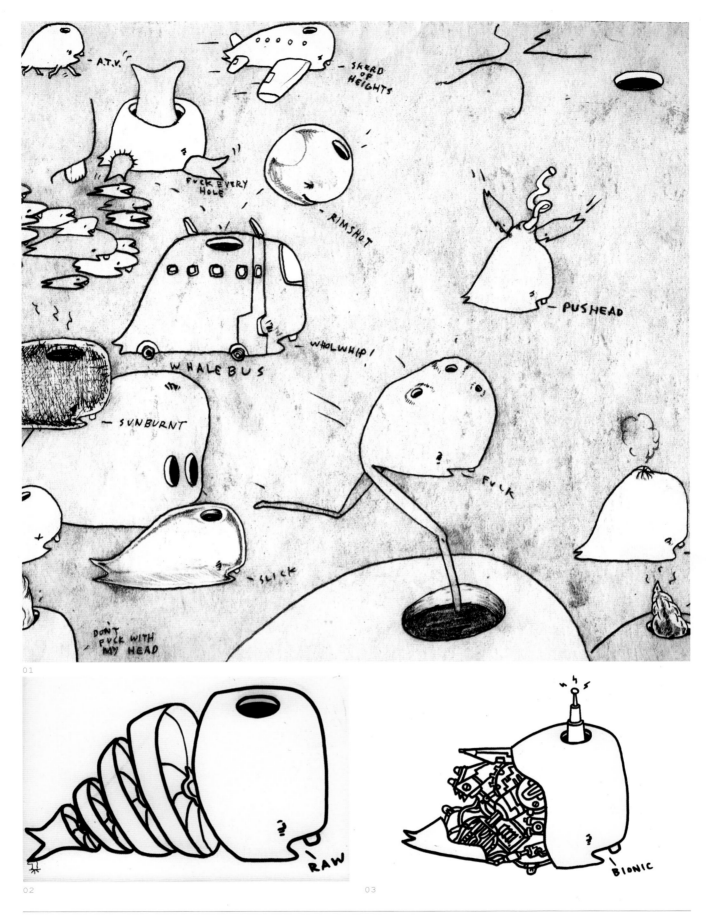

01

02

03

04

01-04 Mark Rigney

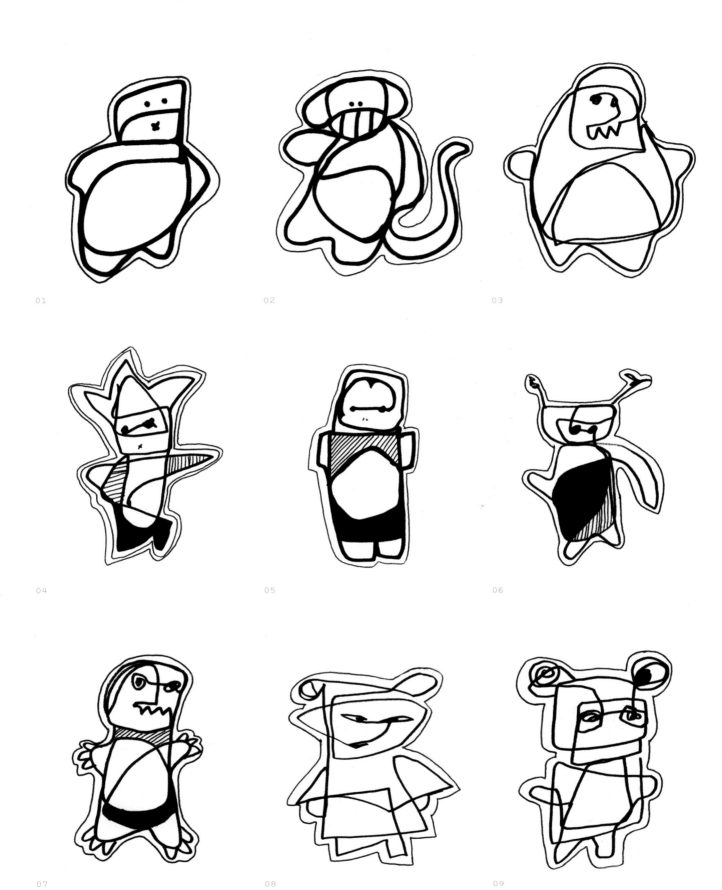

01   02   03

04   05   06

07   08   09

01-09 Mark Rigney

01

02

03

04

05

06

07

08

09

01-06 Jon Burgerman | 07-09 Rina Donnersmarck

01-02 Adam Neate

01 Syrup | 02-03 Dino Miyo Alberto | 04 Crashcarcity

01

02   03   04

01-04 Dino Miyo Alberto

Ohyun Kwon

Ohyun Kwon

01   02   03   04   05   06

07   08   09   10   11   12

13   14   15   16   17   18

19   20   21   22   23   24

25   26   27   28   29   30

31   32   33   34   35   36

01–18 Mr. Jago | 19–36 Rina Donnersmarck

01   02   03

04   05   06   07   08   09

10   11   12   13   14   15

16   17   18   19   20   21

22   23   24   25   26   27

01-04 Bufalo Club | 05 Raoul Deleo | 06 Corey Barba | 07-09 Eighty-John / Maya Maxx
10-15 Unit9 | 16 Jake | 17-18 Jakob Kanior | 19-21 Love Ablan | 22-27 Corey Barba

JACKSON

01

02

01 Jakob Kanior | 02 Makak

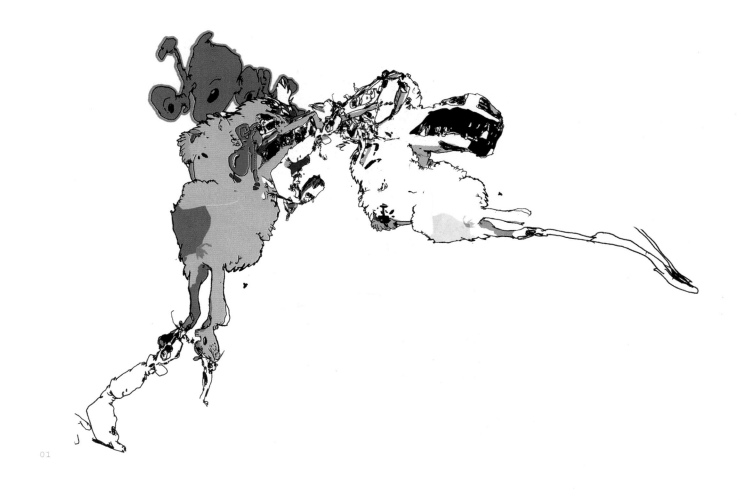

01

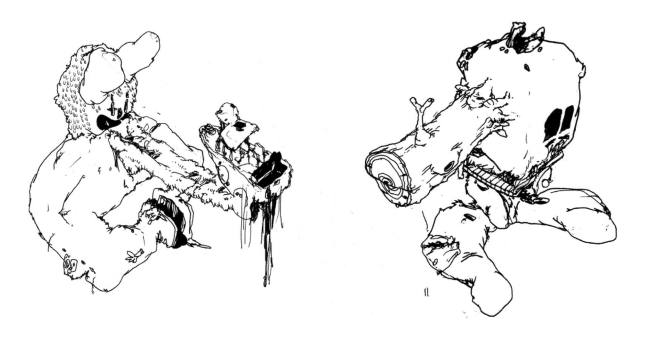

02

03

01-03 Dan Sparkes

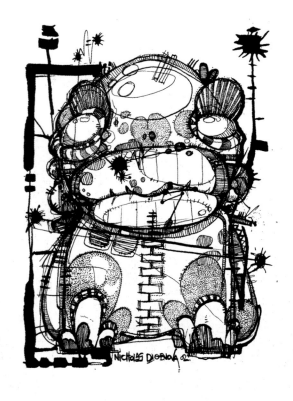

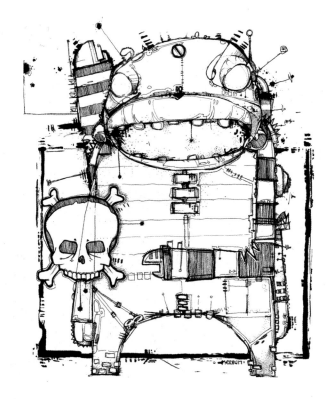

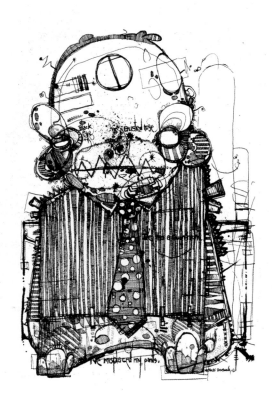

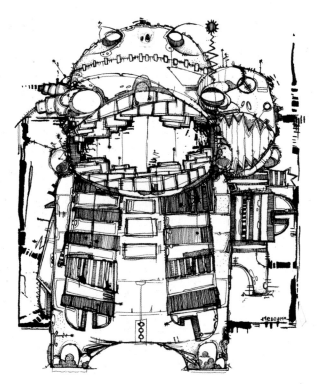

01-04 Nicholas Di Genova

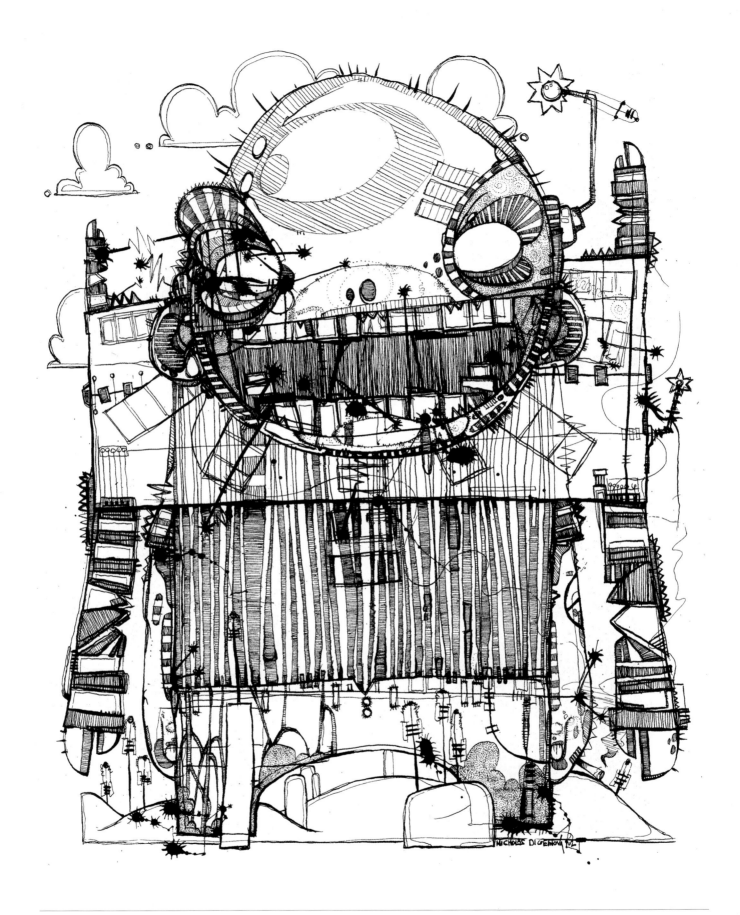

Nicholas Di Genova

01-03 Mysterious Al | 04 Mr. Jago

01 Mokë | 02 Michiko Stehrenberger | 03 Mokë | 04-06 Makak | 07-09 Travis Pendlebury

01

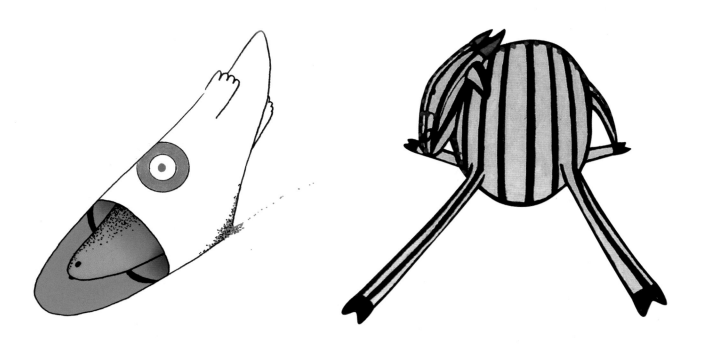

01-02 FriendsWithYou | 03 Zookeeper / Meish

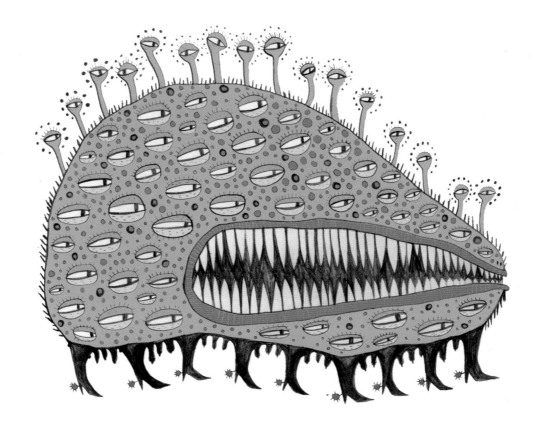

01

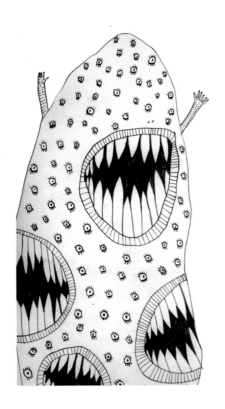

02

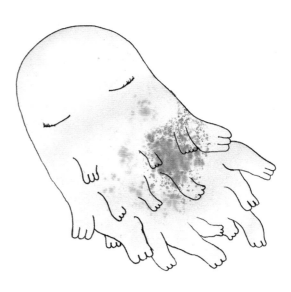

03

01-02 Rina Donnersmarck | 03 FriendsWithYou

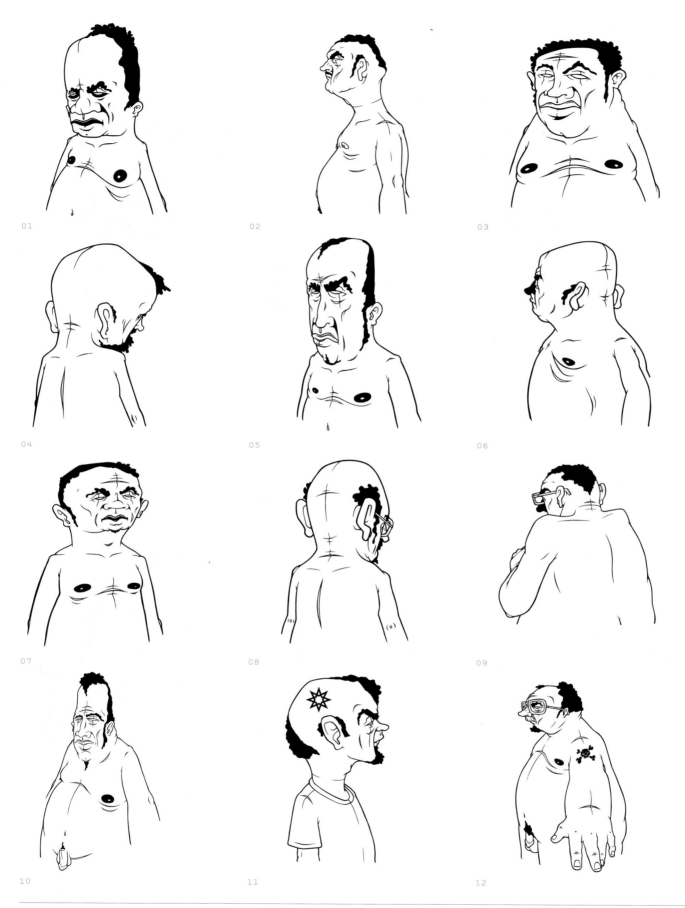

01

02

03

04

05

06

07

08

09

10

11

12

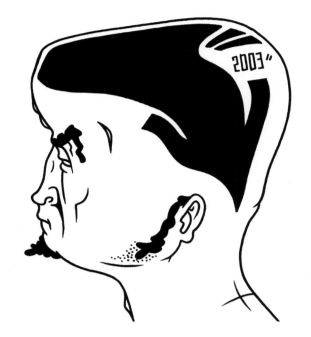

01

02

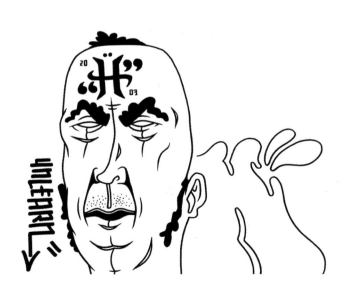

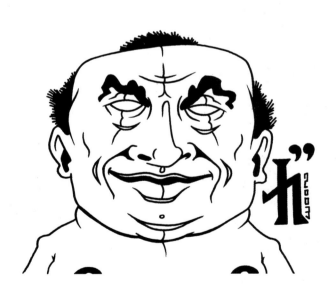

03

04

01

03

01-02 Dino Miyo Alberto

01

02

03

01-03 Dino Miyo Alberto

Finsta, Killah & Mabe

Finsta & Killah

5

STREET ART

The street can be used as a publishing medium. Today's street art represents a number of influences coming together, and characters are an indispensable element here. Even in the mid-Eighties, graffiti artists were developing characters. Most of them overdrew their scene's particular recognition features (spray cans, peaked caps, Adidas sportswear, necklaces, etc.) to the point of caricature. As the figures were executed using the sprayer's special tools (can, paint roller and marker), they quickly started to look unmistakable.

The word caricature comes from character. A caricature is intended to exaggerate the most striking features of the person represented. It takes a great deal of time to portray individuals on the walls of buildings as accurately as possible, and it is usually illegal. For this reason such caricatures were simplified technically, or the image was prepared on paper and then applied to the wall in seconds. There are examples of both techniques in the book. Posters or stickers are often used to publish characters as trademarks. Often the same figures occur frequently in an artist's hometown, or in particularly exposed places in a strange one.

Something that plays a part here is the fact that street art has largely detached itself from the classic graffiti context. The redundancy of the tag in the cityscape has blunted viewers' vision. One tag on a pure white wall is striking. One tag among forty others on the same wall isn't striking at all. Then again, a single clear character among the forty tags will stand out.

This is why a lot of people exclude themselves from the traditionalist graffiti context, and a lot of people now do character-based street art who come from the comic or the art scene.

It seems as though the various scenes are mingling with each other a great deal and the street has taken its place as a medium or a stage on an equal footing with galleries or museums, and publication in books and magazines. It is in fact street presence that first makes a character by a certain artist or designer into a trademark. These trademarks are being quoted in the relevant fashion advertising for scene products, or finding their way into art galleries and museums more and more frequently and rapidly.

01

02

03

01 Géza Nyíry | 02 Esm - Artificial | 03 Igit

01 The London Police | 02 Buffmonster | 03-04 Igit | 05 Kaori Hamura

01

02

01-02 Flying Fortress

01

02

01-02 Alëxone

01-02 Alëxone

01

02

03

01-02 Boris Hoppek | 03 Igit

01-02 D*Face | 03 Invader | 04 Jake | 05 East Eric | 06 Sofuzzycrew

01

02

03

01-02 Adam Cruickshank | 03 D*Face / The London Police

01

02

03

01 Felipe Yung | 02 Buffmonster | 03 Dave Warnke

01

02

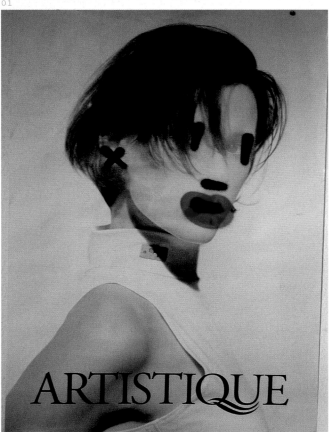

03

ARTISTIQUE

04

05

01-03 Boris Hoppek | 04-05 Dan Sparkes

01-03 Boris Hoppek | 04 D*Face

01

02

03

01 PictoOrphanage | 02-03 Finsta

01-02 Finsta | 03 Flying Fortress | 04 Buffmonster

6

ENCYCLOPEDIA

Some motifs keep resurfacing in the works of character designers. Bears and pandas, rabbits or dogs for example, are not just an expression of zeitgeist, but also suitable exercises for different design approaches. Cross-references are exemplary for the possibilities offered by the various techniques.

01 Jakob Kanior | 02 Akroe | 03 Marimo.Craft / Hory's | 04 Superdeux | 05 Ringirl |
06 Maria Pia | 07 Aranzi Aronzo | 08 Sofuzzycrew | 09 Meomi Design | 10 Be@rbrick™ © 2001-2003
Medicom Toy Corporation. All rights reserved. | 11 Grace Montemar | 12 Mori Chack / Pony Canyon
13-14 Sony Communication Network Corporation | 15 Soppcollective | 16 Buffmonster

01   02   03   04

05   06   07   08

09   10   11.   12

13   14   15   16

01-02 Unit9 | 03-04 Benjamin von Eckartsberg | 05 Evalien Lang | 06-07 Mari-chan
08 Crashcarcity | 09-10 Yukinori Dehara | 11 Jum | 12 Mari-chan | 13 Cubemen | 14 Sebastiaan
Van Doninck | 15 Tsai-Fi | 16 Rina Donnersmarck

01   02   03   04

05   06   07   08

09   10   11   12

13   14   15   16

01 Cubemen | 02 Jake | 03 Love Ablan | 04 Mari-chan | 05 Unit9 | 06 Raoul Deleo
07-10 Mari-chan | 11 Dino Miyo Alberto | 12 Mari-chan | 13 Rinzen | 14 Jakob Kanior
15 Mari-chan | 16 Unit9

01

02

03

04

05

THOM
YORKE

06

07

08

HELLO KISSY

FLASHBACK

ADRESS INDEX

WORK INDEX
PAGES 14–68

IMPRINT

INDEX

Pictoplasma 2 by Peter Thaler
Edited by Robert Klanten, Nicolas Bourquin
Layout and Design by Nicolas Bourquin and Mika Mischler
Chapter Photos by Nicolas Bourquin and Mikati
Cover Design by Mika Mischler
Plasma-C Font by Mika Mischler

Prologue "About Japanese character culture" by Takashi Murakami
Translated by AYA
Prologue "Character assassinations"
by Philip Hunt
Preface by Peter Thaler and Lars Denicke
Translated by Michael Robinson

Proofreading by Helga Beck
Production Management by Janni Milstrey
Production Assistance by Katja Haub
Editorial Support Japan by Junko Tozaki

Published by Die Gestalten Verlag, Berlin
Printed by Preses Nams, Riga
Made in Europe

Bibliographic information published by Die Deutsche Bibliothek.
Die Deutsche Bibliothek lists this publication in the Deutsche
Nationalbibliografie; detailed bibliographic data is available in the
Internet at http://dnb.ddb.de.

ISBN 3-89955-021-8

For more information on dgv please check out:
www.die-gestalten.de

Respect copyright, encourage creativity.

741.6 Tha

337128

15

15/02/16